THE SECRET OF
SPIRITUAL
STRENGTH

THE SECRET OF
SPIRITUAL
STRENGTH

ANDREW MURRAY

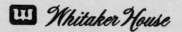

All Scripture quotations are from the *King James Version* (KJV) of the Bible.

THE SECRET OF SPIRITUAL STRENGTH

ISBN: 0-88368-305-9
Printed in the United States of America
Copyright © 1997 by Whitaker House

Whitaker House
30 Hunt Valley Circle
New Kensington, PA 15068

No part of this book may be reproduced or transmitted in any form or by any means, electronic or mechanical, including photocopying, recording, or by any information storage and retrieval system, without permission in writing from the publisher.

2 3 4 5 6 7 8 9 10 11 12 / 07 06 05 04 03 02 01 00 99 98

Contents

One

Knowing Jesus

Knowing Jesus

Their eyes were opened, and they knew him.
—Luke 24:31

It is very possible to have Jesus Himself with you and not know it. It is very possible to listen to all the truth about Jesus, and even to preach about it, and yet not know Him. This fact has made a deep impression on me.

That was the case of the disciples who met Jesus on the road to Emmaus after He was resurrected. Their hearts burned within them as they talked with Him about all the events of His crucifixion and the reports of His resurrection. These disciples spent a very blessed time with Jesus, but if they had gone away before He revealed Himself that evening, they never would have been sure that it was Jesus, for they had been prevented from recognizing Him.

This, I am sorry to say, is the condition of a great number of people in the church of Christ. They know that Christ has risen from the dead. They believe in Him; they frequently have blessed experiences that come from the risen Christ. Very often, at a Bible conference or in a time of silent Bible reading or when God gives His grace to them in a special way, their hearts burn. Yet, it can be said of many Christians, whose hearts are burning within them, that they do not know it is Jesus Himself who is with them.

If you were to ask me what great blessing we should seek from God, my answer would be this: Not only should we think about Jesus Himself and speak about Him and believe in Him, but we should come to the point at which the disciples in the text arrived: *"They knew him."* Everything is to be found in that.

Four Stages of the Christian Life

In the story of the disciples on the road to Emmaus, I recognize four stages of the Christian life. First, there is the stage of the sad and troubled heart. Then there is the time in which the heart is slow to believe. This is followed by the period of the burning heart. But the highest level we are to reach is the stage of the satisfied heart.

The Sad and Troubled Heart

Imagine how the disciples were feeling that morning as they started on their journey. Their hearts were sad and troubled because they thought that Jesus was dead. They did not know that He was alive, and this is the way it is with a large number of Christians. They look to the Cross and they struggle to trust Christ, but they have never yet learned the blessedness of believing that there is a living Christ who will do everything for them. The words that the angel spoke to the women who came to Christ's tomb on the morning of the Resurrection were striking: *"Why seek ye the living among the dead?"* (Luke 24:5). What is the difference between a dead Christ, whom the women had gone to anoint, and a living Christ? The difference is that I must do everything for a dead Christ, but a living Christ does everything for me.

The disciples began the morning with a sad heart. It is very possible that they had spent a sleepless night. What a terrible disappointment they had experienced. They had hoped that Christ would be the Deliverer of

Israel, yet they had seen Him die an accursed death. Their bitter sadness cannot possibly be expressed. Again, the life of many Christians is much the same. They try to believe in Jesus and to trust Him and to hope in Him, but they have no joy. Why? They do not know that there is a living Christ who can be revealed to them.

Slow to Believe

The second stage is taken from the words that Christ spoke to the disciples when He told them that they were *"slow of heart to believe"* (Luke 24:25). They had heard the message from the women, and they told the Stranger who walked with them:

> Certain women also of our company made us astonished, which were early at the sepulchre; and when they found not his body, they came, saying, that they had also seen a vision of angels, which said that he was alive.   (Luke 15:22–23)

And Christ replied to them, *"O fools, and slow of heart to believe"* (v. 25). Yes, there are many Christians today who have heard the Gospel and who know that they must not only believe in a crucified Christ but in a living

12

Christ, and they try to grasp it and take it in, but it does not bring them a blessing. Why? They do not receive the blessing because they want to *feel* it and not to *believe* it. They want to work for it and to receive it through their own efforts, instead of just quietly humbling themselves and believing that Christ, the living Jesus, will do everything for them.

Therefore, that is the second stage. The first stage is one of ignorance, and the second stage is one of unbelief. The doubting heart cannot take in the wonderful truth that Jesus lives.

The Burning Heart

The third stage of the Christian life is the burning heart stage. Jesus came to the two disciples, and after He had reproved them, He began to interpret the Scriptures for them and to tell them of all the wonderful things the prophets had taught. Then their eyes were opened, and they began to understand the Scriptures. They saw that it was true that it had been prophesied that Christ must rise. And as the Living Risen One talked, a mighty spiritual power emanated from Him. It rested upon them, and they began to feel their hearts burn with joy and gladness.

You may be saying, "This is the final stage at which we need to arrive." Yet, God forbid that you should stop there. You may arrive at this third stage, and yet something will still be lacking: the revelation of Christ. The disciples had had a blessed experience of His divine power, but He had not revealed Himself. Our hearts often burn within us at Bible conferences, in churches, in meetings, and in blessed fellowship with God's people. These are precious experiences of the working of God's grace and Spirit, and yet there is something lacking. What is it?

Jesus Himself has been working in us and the power of His risen life has touched us, but we have not been able to say, "I have met Him. He has made Himself known to me." There is a great difference between a burning heart, which becomes cold after a while, and which comes and goes, and the blessed revelation of Jesus Himself as my Savior who takes charge of me and blesses me and keeps me every day!

The Satisfied Heart

The final stage, which I have just described, is the stage of the satisfied heart. I pray that you will arrive at this stage. I am sure that you are praying for this, as well. I am certainly praying that I will arrive at this stage in my own life. Lord Jesus, may we know You in Your divine glory as the Risen One, our Jesus, our Beloved, and our Mighty One.

How to Know Jesus

If you are sad and unable to comprehend or accept this, and if you are saying, "I have never yet known the joy of faith," read the following words carefully, because I am going to tell you how you can know it. Everything centers around one thing. Just as a little child lives day by day in the arms of his mother and grows up year after year under his mother's loving eye, it is possible for you to live every day and hour of your life in fellowship with the Holy Jesus. Let your sad heart begin to hope. You may be asking, "Will He really reveal Himself?" He did it for the disciples, and He will do it for you.

Perhaps you have arrived at the stage of the burning heart and can relate many blessed experiences that you have had, but somehow there is a worm at the root. The experiences do not last and your heart is very changeable. Come, beloved believer, and follow Christ. Say, "Jesus, reveal Yourself so that I may know You personally. I am not only asking to drink the living water, I want the Fountain. I am not only asking to bathe myself in the light, I want the *'Sun of righteousness'* (Mal. 4:2) within my heart. I am not only asking to know You, who have touched me and warmed my heart and blessed me, but I want to know that I have the unchangeable Jesus dwelling within my heart and remaining with me forever."

It may be that you have gotten beyond the stage of the sad heart, but you still feel that you do not have what you want. If you will throw open your heart and give up everything, except believing and allowing Him to do what He wants, it will come. Praise God, it will come!

To Whom Does Jesus Reveal Himself?

The main question I want to address is, What are the conditions under which our blessed Lord reveals Himself? Or, to put it another way, To whom will Jesus reveal Himself? We find the answer in the way Jesus responded to the disciples on the road to Emmaus.

Those Who Give Up Everything for Him

First of all, I think we can conclude from our text that Christ revealed Himself to those

16

disciples who had given up everything for Him. He had said to them, *"Deny* [yourself], *and take up* [your] *cross, and follow me"* (Matt. 16:24), and they had done it. With all their unfaithfulness and with all their weaknesses, they had followed Christ to the end. He had said to them,

> *Ye are they which have continued with me in my temptations. And I appoint unto you a kingdom, as my Father hath appointed unto me.* (Luke 22:28–29)

They were not perfect men, but they would have died for Him. They had loved Him, obeyed Him, followed Him. They had left everything, and for three years they had been following Christ earnestly. You say, "Tell me what Christ wants from me so that I may have His wonderful presence. Tell me the kind of person to whom Christ will reveal Himself in this highest and fullest way." My answer is, "He will reveal Himself to the one who is ready to give up everything and to follow Him." If Christ is to give Himself wholly to me, He must know that I am wholly committed to Him. I trust that God will give us grace, so that these words I have written about consecration and surrender—not only of all evil, but of many lawful things, and even, if necessary, of life itself—may lead us to understand the demand that Jesus makes upon us.

A motto that is often quoted is, "God first." In one sense, that is a beautiful motto, and yet I am not always satisfied with it because it is a motto that is often misunderstood. "God first" may mean "I" second, something else third, and something else fourth. In this hierarchy, God is first in order, but He still is one of a series of authorities, and that is not the place God wants. The true meaning of the phrase, "God first," is "God all, God everything," and this is what Christ wants. To be willing to give up everything, to submit to Christ so that He may teach you what to say and what to do, is the first characteristic of the person to whom Christ will come. Are you ready to take this step and to say, "Jesus, I do give up everything. Now that I have surrendered to You, I ask You to reveal Yourself"?

Do not hesitate to do this. Speak it from your heart, and let this be the time in which a new sacrifice is laid at the feet of the blessed Lamb of God.

Those Convicted of Their Unbelief

The first step is to turn away from everything else and to follow Him, to give up everything in submission to Him and just live a life of simple love and obedience. But there is a second thing that is needed in a person who is to have this full revelation of Christ: he must be convicted of his unbelief.

"O fools, and slow of heart to believe all that the prophets have spoken" (Luke 24:25). If we could only see the amount of unbelief in the hearts of God's children, which bars the doors of their hearts, closing them against Christ, we would be astonished and ashamed! Yet, where there is faith instead of unbelief, Christ cannot help coming in. He cannot help coming where there is a living faith. When the heart is opened and prepared, when it is full of faith, then Christ will come as naturally as water runs into a hollow place.

What is it that continues to hinder some earnest believers who say, "I have given myself to the Lord Jesus. I have done it often, and by His grace I am doing it every day. God knows how earnestly and genuinely I am doing it. I have the assurance of God's Word, and I know God has blessed me"? Even though they are trying to yield to God, they are hindered because they have not been convicted of their unbelief. *"O fools, and slow of heart to believe."*

Do you want the Lord Jesus to give you a full revelation of Himself? Are you willing to acknowledge that you are a fool for never having believed in Him? Then pray, "Lord Jesus, it is my own fault. You are right here, longing to have possession of me. You have always been here with Your faithful promises, waiting to reveal Yourself."

Have you ever heard of a person who did not long to make himself known to someone he loved? Christ longs to reveal Himself to us, but He cannot do so because of our unbelief. May God convict us of this unbelief so that we may become utterly ashamed and broken down, and cry out to Him, "Oh, my God, what is this unbelief that actually throws a barrier across the door of my heart so that Christ cannot come in, that blinds my eyes so that I cannot see Jesus, even though He is so near? He has been near me for ten or twenty years, and from time to time He has given me a burning heart. I have enjoyed the experience of a little of His love and grace, and yet I have not had the revelation of Him in which He takes possession of my heart and remains with me in unbroken communion."

Oh, may God convict us of unbelief. Let us make sure that we believe, because *all things are possible to him that believeth* (Mark 9:23). This is God's promise, and the blessing of receiving the revelation of Jesus can come only to those who learn to believe and trust Him.

Those Who Persevere in Seeking the Revelation

There is another characteristic of those to whom this special revelation of Christ will come: they do not rest until they obtain it. When the disciples were talking with Jesus on the road to Emmaus, their hearts were burning. As they drew close to their destination, Christ acted as if He were going farther. He put them to the test, and if they had allowed Him to go on quietly, if they had been content with the experience of the burning heart, they would have lost something infinitely better. But they were not content with it. They were not content to go home to the other disciples that night and say, "What a blessed afternoon we have had. What wonderful teaching we have had!" No. The burning heart and the blessed experience made them say, "Sir, *'abide with us'*" (Luke 24:29), and they compelled Him to come in with them.

This always reminds me of the story of Jacob, who wrestled with a man all night and then said, *"I will not let thee go, except thou bless me"* (Gen. 32:26). This is the quality that prepares us for the revelation of Jesus. My dear friend, has this been the attitude in which you have looked upon the wonderful blessing of the presence of Jesus? Have you said: "My

Lord Jesus, though I do not understand it, though I cannot grasp it, though my struggles do not accomplish anything, I am not going to let You go. If it is possible for a sinner on earth to have You dwelling in his heart in resurrection power every day, every hour, and every moment—shining within him, filling him with love and joy—then I want it"? Is that truly what you want? Then come and say, "Lord Jesus, I cannot let You go unless You bless me."

The Need for a Revelation of Christ

The question is often asked, What is the reason for the weak spiritual lives of so many Christians? This is an excellent question, for it is remarkable how little the church responds to Christ's call, how little the church is what Christ wants her to be. What really is the matter? What actually is needed? Various answers may be given, but there is one answer that includes them all: each believer needs the full revelation of a personal Christ as an indwelling Lord, as a satisfying portion.

When the Lord Jesus was here on earth, what was it that distinguished His disciples from other people? The answer is that Jesus took them away from their fishnets and their homes. He gathered them around Himself, and they knew Him. He was their Master; He guarded them, and they followed Him. And what is supposed to make the difference today between Christ's disciples—not those who are just hoping to get to heaven, but Christ's wholehearted disciples—and other people? It is this: fellowship with Jesus every hour of the day. When Christ was on earth, He was able to keep the disciples with Him for three years, day after day. Now that Christ is in heaven, He is able to do what He could not do when He was on earth—to keep in the closest fellowship with every believer throughout the whole world. Praise God for this.

You may know the verse in Ephesians: *"He that descended is the same also that ascended up far above all heavens, that he might fill all things"* (4:10). Why was our Lord Jesus taken up to heaven, away from the life of earth? He ascended to heaven because the life of earth is confined to localities, but the life of heaven has no limits, no boundaries, and no localities. Christ was taken up to heaven so that, in the power of God, the omnipresent God, He might be able to fill every one of His followers on earth and be with every individual believer in a personal way.

This is what my heart wants to experience by faith. It is a possibility, it is a promise, it is my birthright, and I want to have it. By the grace of God, I want to say, "Jesus, I will not rest until You have revealed Yourself fully to me."

Often, people have very blessed experiences during the stage of the burning heart. One of the major characteristics of that stage is that believers delight in God's Word. How did the disciples get their burning hearts? It was through the way in which Christ opened the Scriptures to them. He made it all look different and new, and they saw what they had never seen before. They could not help feeling how wonderful and how heavenly the teaching was.

There are many Christians who discover that the best time of the day is when they can read and explore their Bibles, and they love nothing more than to get a new spiritual insight. As a person who mines diamonds rejoices when he has found a diamond, or someone who digs for gold when he has found a nugget, they delight when they get some new thought from the Bible, and they feed upon it. Yet, even with all their interest in God's Word, and with all the joy that is stirred in their hearts, when they go to their work or attend to their daily duties, they find that there is still something missing in their lives.

From time to time, we must leave all the many and diverse blessings that Jesus gives us, and come to the one blessing that encompasses them all: the blessing that Jesus makes Himself known, that Jesus is *willing* to make Himself known to us. If I were to ask, "Is this not exactly what you and I need, and what many of us have been longing for?" I am sure you would answer, "Yes, this is what I want!" Think of the blessedness that will come from it.

> Oh, the peace my Savior gives!
> Peace I never knew before,
> And my way has brighter grown,
> Since I've learnt to trust Him more.

I recently had a letter from someone who wrote what a wonderful comfort and strength the above poem had been in the midst of difficulties and troubles. However, how can a person *maintain* peace in his life? It was the presence of Christ that brought the peace; therefore, peace must be sustained through the continual presence of Jesus. Remember that when the storm on the sea was threatening to swallow up the disciples, it was the presence of Christ Himself that brought the peace.

Do you want peace and rest? Then you must have Jesus Himself. You talk of purity, you talk of cleansing, you talk of deliverance from sin. Praise God, the deliverance and the cleansing come when the living Jesus comes and gives power. Then you have the resurrected Christ, the heavenly Christ who sits on the throne, making Himself known to you. Surely this is the secret of purity and the secret of strength.

The Need for a Friendship with Jesus

Where does the strength of so many believers come from? It comes from the joy of a personal friendship with Jesus. If those disciples had gone back with their burning hearts to the other disciples, they could have told them wonderful things about a man who had explained the Scriptures and the promises to them, but they could not have said, "We have seen Jesus." They might have said, "Jesus is alive—we are sure of that," but that would not have satisfied the others. Yet, now they could go back and say, "We have seen Jesus Himself. He has revealed Himself to us."

Most believers are happy to work for Christ; however, there is a common complaint throughout the church, from the ministers in the pulpit to the least-noticed Christian workers, of a lack of joy and a lack of experiencing the blessings of God. Let us try to find out whether or not the secret of joy may be found where the Lord Jesus comes and shows Himself to us as our Master, and then speaks to us. When you have Jesus with you, and when you take every step with the thought that it is Jesus who wants you to go, that it is Jesus who sends you and is helping you, then there will be brightness in your testimony. Your experience will help other believers, and they will begin to understand, too. They will say, "I see why I have failed. I received the Word, I received the blessing, and I thought I was living the life of Christ, but I did not allow the living Jesus to be a constant, daily presence in my life."

Perhaps you may now be asking, "How will this revelation of Christ come?" That is the secret that no one can know, that Jesus keeps to Himself. It will come in the power of the Holy Spirit. The disciples on the road to Emmaus had a revelation of the living, risen Christ. The Scripture says, *"They knew him."* He revealed Himself, and then He vanished from their sight.

Was that vision of Christ worth much? It was gone in a moment, yet it was worth heaven, eternity, everything. Why? From that time on, Christ's disciples were no longer to relate to Him in an earthly way. From then on, Christ was to live in the life of heaven. When Christ was resurrected, He entered into a new life. His resurrection life is entirely different from what His life had been before His death. He is now in the power of the Spirit who fills heaven, in the power of the Spirit who is the power of the Godhead, in the power of the Spirit who fills our hearts.

Thank God, Christ can reveal Himself to each one of us by the power of the Holy Spirit. Yet, how He does so is a secret thing between Christ and each individual believer. Take this assurance, *"Their eyes were opened, and they knew him,"* and believe that it was written for you.

You may be able to say, "I have known the other three stages. I have experienced the stage of the sad heart, when I mourned that I did not know the living Christ; I have known the stage of the heart that is slow to believe, when I struggled with my lack of faith; and I now know the stage of the burning heart, in which I experience great times of joy and blessedness."

If you can say that, then come and know the stage of the satisfied heart. You will have a heart that has been made glad for eternity, a heart that cannot keep in its joy but goes back to other believers, as the disciples went back to the believers in Jerusalem, and says, "It is true. Jesus has revealed Himself. I know it. I feel it."

Beloved, how will this revelation come? Jesus will tell you. Just come to the Lord Jesus and say a simple, childlike prayer. You need to come to Jesus yourself. My work is done. I have pointed you to the Lamb of God, to the Risen One. You must now enter into the presence of the Holy One and begin to plead, "Oh, Savior, I have come so that I might have this blessedness with me at all times—Jesus Himself, my portion forever."

Two

The Secret of the Christian Life

The Secret of the Christian Life

*Lo, I am with you alway, even unto the
end of the world.*
—Matthew 28:20

I am aware of the many struggles, difficulties, and failures of which many Christians complain, and I know that many are trying to make a new effort to begin a holy life. I know that their hearts are continually afraid that they might fail again, because they experience so many difficulties and temptations, and because of the natural weakness of their characters. My heart longs to be able to tell them the secret of the Christian life in words so simple that a little child could understand them.

But even so, I ask myself, "Can I venture to hope that I will be able to describe the glorious, heavenly Lord Jesus to these believers so that they can see Him in His glory? Can I open their eyes to see that there is a divine, almighty Christ who does actually come into people's hearts, who faithfully promises, *'If a man love me, he will keep my words: and my Father will love him, and we will come unto him, and make our abode with him'* (John 14:23) and, *'I will never leave thee, nor forsake thee'"* (Heb. 13:5)? No, my words are not adequate for that.

However, my Lord Jesus can use me, as a simple servant, to encourage and help struggling Christians. I can say, "I urge you to come into the presence of Jesus and to wait on Him, and He will reveal Himself to you." I pray that God may use His precious Word to encourage you in this.

The secret of the Christian's strength and joy is simply the presence of the Lord Jesus. When Christ was on earth, He was physically present with His disciples. They walked about together all day, and at night they met together and often ate together and stayed at the same house. They were continually together. The presence of Jesus was the training school of His disciples. They were united to Him by that wonderful communion of love for three long years; in their fellowship with Christ, they learned to know Him, and He instructed and corrected them and prepared them for what they were to receive at a later time. After His resurrection, just before He ascended to heaven, He said to them, *"Lo, I am with you alway* [all the days], *even unto the end of the world."*

What a promise! Christ was with Peter in the boat, and Christ sat with John at the Last Supper, yet I can have Christ with me in just as real a way. In fact, I can have Him in a more complete way, for, before Christ's resurrection, they knew Him as a human being, an individual who was separate from them, but I may know Christ as the One who is glorified in the power of the throne of God—the omnipotent Christ, the omnipresent Christ.

Yes, what a promise! You may be asking, "How is this possible?" My answer is, "It is possible because Christ is God and because Christ, after having been made a human being, went up into the throne and life of God. And now, that blessed Christ Jesus, with His loving, pierced heart; that blessed Christ Jesus, who lived on earth; that same Christ who was glorified into the glory of God, can be in me and can be with me every day.

You may be saying, "Is having the constant presence of the Lord Jesus really possible for someone in business or for someone who has the responsibility of a large and demanding household or for a poor man who is occupied with his problems? Is it possible? Can I always be thinking of Jesus?" Thank God, you do not need to be constantly thinking of Him. You may be the manager of a bank, and your whole attention may be required to carry out the business that you have to do. However, while you have to think of your business, Jesus will think of you, and He will come in and will take charge of you.

When a three-month-old baby sleeps in his mother's arms, he lies there helplessly. He hardly knows his mother; he does not think of her, but the mother thinks of the child. And this is the blessed mystery of love: Jesus, the God-man, waits to come to me in the greatness of His love, and when He gets possession of my heart, He embraces me in those divine arms and tells me, "My child, I, the Faithful One, I, the Mighty One, will remain with you. I will watch over you and keep you every day." He tells me that He will come into my heart so that I can be a happy Christian, a holy Christian, a useful Christian. You say, "Oh, if only I could believe that, if only I could believe that it is possible to have Christ constantly taking and keeping charge of me every hour and every moment!"

Yet, this is exactly my message to you. When Jesus said to His disciples, *"Lo, I am with you alway,"* He meant it in the fullness of the divine omnipresence, in the fullness of the divine love, and He longs to reveal Himself to you and to me as we have never seen Him before.

And now, just think for a moment what a blessed life it must be to have the continual presence of Jesus. Is that not the secret of peace and happiness? Many people are saying, "If I could just arrive at the point at which every day and all day I believed that Jesus was watching over me and continually keeping me. What peace I would have in the thought, 'I have no care if He cares for me, and I have no fear if He provides for me.'"

Your heart says that this is too good to be true, and that it is too glorious to be possible for you. Still, you acknowledge that it must be a very blessed way to live. Fearful one, mistaken one, anxious one, I bring you God's promise; it is for me and for you. Jesus will do it. As God, He is able, and Jesus is willing and longing as the Crucified One to keep you in perfect peace. This is a wonderful fact, and it is the secret of unspeakable joy.

This is also the secret of holiness. Instead of indwelling sin, there is an indwelling Christ who conquers it. Instead of indwelling sin, there is the indwelling life and light and love of the blessed Son of God. He is the secret of holiness.

Christ *"is made unto us...sanctification"* (1 Cor. 1:30).

Always remember that it is Christ Himself who is our holiness. The experience of having Christ come into you, take charge of your whole being, rule all things—your nature and your thoughts and your will and your emotions—will make you holy. Christians talk about holiness, but do you know what holiness is? You have as much of holiness as you have of Christ, for it is written, *"Both he that sanctifieth and they who are sanctified are all of one"* (Heb. 2:11). Christ sanctifies us by bringing God's life into us.

We read in Judges, *"The spirit of the LORD came upon Gideon"* (6:34); that is, Gideon was clothed with the Spirit. But in the New Testament there is an equally wonderful text in which we read, *"Put ye on the Lord Jesus Christ"* (Rom. 13:14). We are to clothe ourselves with Christ Jesus. What does this mean? It does not only mean that we are given a righteousness outside of ourselves, but that we are to clothe ourselves with the living character of the living Christ, with the living love of the living Christ.

Put On the Lord Jesus

This is a tremendous calling. I cannot put on Christ unless I believe and understand that

I have to put Him on like a garment that covers my whole being. I have to put on a living Christ who has said, *"Lo, I am with you always."* Just pull the folds of that robe of light closer around you, the robe with which Christ wants to dress you. Just acknowledge that Christ is with you, on you, in you. Be clothed with Christ completely!

Examine one characteristic of His after another, and hear God's word, *"Let this mind be in you, which was also in Christ Jesus"* (Phil. 2:5). This passage of Scripture tells you that He was obedient to the point of death. When you respond and put on this Jesus, then you have received and put on Christ the Obedient One, Christ whose whole life was obedience. He becomes your life, and His obedience rests upon you until you learn to whisper, as Jesus did, *"My Father...thy will be done"* (Matt. 26:42) and, *"Lo, I come to do thy will, O God"* (Heb. 10:9).

This, too, is the secret of power for witness and work. Why is it so difficult to be obedient, and why do we sin so often? People sing, "Oh, to be wholly Yours," and they sing it from their hearts. Then why are they disobedient again? Where does the disobedience come from? They are disobedient because they are trying to obey a distant Christ, and therefore

His commands do not come to them with power.

What does God's Word tell us about all this? When God wanted to send any man to do His will, He met with him and talked with him and encouraged him, time after time. God appeared to Abraham seven or eight times, and gave him one command after another. In this way, Abraham learned to obey Him perfectly. God appeared to Joshua and to Gideon, and they obeyed. Why are we not obedient? It is because we have so little of this close communion with Jesus.

However, if we knew the blessed, heavenly secret of having the presence of Christ with us every day, every hour, every minute, what a joy it would be to obey! We could not live with the conscious thought, "My Lord Jesus is with me and around me," and not obey Him. Are you beginning to long for this and to say, "I must have the ever abiding presence of Jesus"?

There are some Christians who try not to be disobedient, who serve God very faithfully on Sundays and during the week, who pray for grace and blessing, but who complain that they have very little blessing and power. Why? They are not allowing the living Jesus to fill their hearts completely.

I sometimes think of this as an extremely solemn truth. There is a great diversity of gifts among ministers and others who teach and preach. However, I am sure of this: a person's gifts are not the measure of his real power. God can see what neither you nor I can see, though sometimes people can sense it to some degree. Yet, to the extent that a person has—not as a feeling or a desire or a thought, but in reality—the very Spirit and presence of Jesus upon him, an unseen silent influence comes out from him. That secret influence is the holy presence of Jesus.

I hope that what I have written to this point has shown you what a desirable thing it is to have the continual presence of Jesus, and what a blessed thing it is to live for. Let me now give you an answer to a question that arises in many people's hearts: "Tell me how I can obtain this blessed, constant presence of Jesus, and how I can always keep it. I think that if I were to have this, I would have everything. The Lord Jesus has come very near to me. I have tried to turn away from everything that can hinder my relationship with my Lord, and He has been very close to me. But how can I know that He will always be with me?"

Continual Belief

My reply to this is, if you were to ask the Lord, "Oh, my blessed Lord Christ, what must

I do? How can I enjoy Your never failing presence?" His first response would be, "Only believe. I have said it often, and you have only partly understood it, but I will say it again. My child, only believe." *even Though our emotions aren't*

We believe by faith. We sometimes speak *There say it...* of faith as trust, and it is a very helpful thing to tell people that faith is trust. However, *I believe* when people say, as they sometimes do, that faith is nothing but trust, that is not the case. *Faith* is a much broader word than *trust*. It is by faith that I learn to know the invisible God, and it is by faith that I see Him. Faith is my spiritual eyesight for what is unseen and heavenly.

You often try hard to trust God, and you fail. Why? It is because you have not first *Every Day!* taken time to see God. How can you trust God fully until you have met Him and until you have come to know Him? You ask, "Where should I begin?" Begin with believing, with presenting yourself before God in an attitude of silent worship and asking Him to let a sense of His greatness and His presence come upon you. You must ask Him to let your heart be covered over with His holy presence. You must seek to know in your heart the presence of an almighty and all-loving God, an unspeakably loving God. Take time to worship Him as the omnipotent God, to feel that the very power that created the world, the very power that raised Jesus from the dead, is working in your heart at this moment.

We do not often experience this because we do not believe. We must take time to believe. Jesus is saying to you, "My child, shut your eyes to the world, and shut out of your heart all your thoughts about religion, and begin to believe in God Himself." That is the true meaning of the first part of the Apostles' Creed, "I believe in God."

By believing, I open my heart to receive this glorious God, and I bow and worship. Then, as I believe in who He is, I look up and see the Lamb on the throne, and I believe that the almighty power of God is in Jesus for the very purpose of revealing His presence to my heart.

Why are there Two on the throne? Is it not enough for God the Father to be there? The Lamb of God is on the throne for our benefit. The Lamb upon the throne is Christ Himself; He has the power, as God, to take possession of us.

Do not think that this will never be a reality for you, or do not think of it as something that is within your reach only for the present moment. Cultivate the habit of faith. Say, "Jesus, I believe in Your glory; I believe in

Your omnipotence; I believe in Your power working within me; I believe in Your living, loving presence with me, revealing itself in divine power."

Do not be occupied with feelings or experiences. You will find it far simpler and easier just to trust and to say, "I am sure He is taking care of me completely." Put yourself aside for the time being. Do not think or speak about yourself, but think about who Jesus is.

And then remember that you are always to believe. I sometimes feel that I cannot find the words to explain that God wants His people to believe from morning until night. Every breath ought to be spent just believing. Yes, it is indeed true; the Lord Jesus loves for us to be continually believing from morning until evening, and you must begin to make that the chief thing in life. In the morning, when you wake up, go out to your day with a strong faith in His presence; and in the watches of the night, let this thought be present with you, "My Savior, Jesus, is around me and near me." At any point of the day or night, you can look to Jesus and say, "I want to trust You always."

You know what trust is. It is so sweet to trust. But now, can you trust Jesus, this Presence, this keeping Presence? He lives for you in heaven. You are marked with His blood, and

He loves you. Can you say, "My King is with me every day"? Trust Jesus to fulfill His own promises.

Continual Obedience

There is a second answer that I think Christ would give if you were to come to Him in faith and say, "Is there anything more, my blessed Master?" I think I can hear His answer: "My child, always obey."

Do not fail to understand the lesson contained in this. You must distinctly and definitely receive the words *obey* and *obedience*, and learn to say for yourself, "Now I have to obey, and by the grace of God I am going to obey in everything."

When Cecil Rhodes was the prime minister of South Africa, he went to an event, thinking he had the amount of the entrance fee in his pocket. When he got to the gate, however, he found that he did not have enough money, and he said to the attendant, "I am Mr. Rhodes. Let me in, and I will make sure that the ticket is paid for." However, the man said, "I cannot help that, sir, I have my orders," and he refused to let Mr. Rhodes in. The prime minister had to borrow the money from a friend and pay the fee before he could go through the gate. At a dinner afterward, Mr.

Rhodes spoke about it, and he said it was a real joy to see a man stick to his orders like that. That is exactly the point I am trying to make. The man had his orders and that was enough for him, and whoever came to the gate had to pay the fee before he could enter. God's children ought to be like soldiers and be ready to say, "I must obey."

What a wonderful thing it would be to have this thought in our hearts: "Jesus, I love to obey You." Personal communion with the Savior will be followed by the joy of personal service and allegiance. Are you ready to obey in all humility and weakness and reverence? Can you say, "Yes, Lord Jesus, I will obey"? If so, give yourself up to Him completely. Then your thinking will be, "I am not going to speak one word if I think that Jesus would not like to hear it. I am not going to have an opinion of my own, but my whole life is going to be covered with the purity of Christ's obedience to the Father and His self-sacrificing love for me. I want Christ to have my whole life, my whole heart, my whole character. I want to be like Christ and to obey." Give yourself up to this loving obedience.

Close Daily Fellowship with Christ

Thirdly, if you were to say, "My Master, Blessed Savior, tell me everything. I will believe, and I will continue to obey. Is there anything more that I need in order to secure the enjoyment of Your continual presence?" I believe this would be His answer: "My child, you need close fellowship with Me every day."

The fault of many who try to obey and try to believe is that they do it in their own strength. They do not know that if the Lord Jesus is to reign in their hearts, they must have close daily communion with Him. You cannot do all that He desires, but Jesus will do it for you. There are many Christians who fail at this point, and for this reason they do not understand what it is to have fellowship with Jesus.

Let me try to impress upon you that God has given you a loving, living Savior, but how can He bless you if you do not meet with Him? The joy of friendship is found in fellowship, and Jesus asks for this fellowship every day so that He may have time to influence you, to tell you of Himself, to teach you, to breathe His Spirit into you, and to give you new life and joy and strength.

And remember, fellowship with Jesus does not mean just spending half an hour or an hour reading your Bible and praying. A person may study his Bible or his Bible commentary carefully, he may look up all the parallel passages in the chapter, and he may be able to tell you all about it, and yet he may never have met Jesus at all during the time that he spent studying. You may be praying for five or ten minutes a day, and yet you may never have met Jesus.

And so, we must remember that, although the Bible is very precious and reading it is very blessed and necessary, Bible reading and prayer, in themselves, are not fellowship with Jesus. What we need is to meet with Jesus every morning and to say, "Lord, here is a new day again, and I am just as weak in myself as I ever was. Please come this morning and feed me with Yourself and speak to my soul." My friend, it is not your faith that will keep you standing, but it is a living Jesus with whom you meet every day in fellowship and worship and love. Wait in His presence, no matter how cold and faithless you feel. Wait before Him, and say, "Lord, helpless as I am, I believe and rest in the blessed assurance that what You have promised, You will do for me."

Work for Jesus

If you were to ask the Master once again, "Lord Jesus, is that all?" His answer would be, "No, my child. There is one thing more."

"And what is that? You have told me to believe and to obey and to stay close to You. What additional thing would You like?"

"Work for Me, my child. Remember, I have redeemed you for My service. I have redeemed you so that I may have a witness to go out into the world and tell others about Me."

Friend, do not hide your spiritual treasure, and do not think that if Jesus is with you, you can hide it. One of two things will happen—either you must give up all of your treasure, or it will have to be revealed. You have perhaps heard of the little girl who, after attending one of evangelist D. L. Moody's meetings, started singing hymns at home. The child's parents were in a good position in society, and when the mother heard the little girl singing hymns in the living room, she forbade her to continue doing so. One day, the girl was singing a hymn with the words, "Oh, I'm so glad that Jesus loves me," and her mother said, "My child, why are you singing this when I have forbidden it?" She replied, "Oh, Mother, I cannot help it. It comes out by itself."

If Jesus Christ is in a person's heart, He will be revealed in the person's life. The reason for this is not only that it is our duty to witness about Him (it *is* our duty, yet it is much more than that), but if you do not tell others about Christ, it is just an indication that you have not given yourself up completely to Jesus: your character, your reputation, your all. It means you are holding back from Him. You must confess Jesus in the world, in your home, and, in fact, everywhere. You know the Lord's command, *"Go ye into all the world, and preach the gospel to every creature"* (Mark 16:15). He has also said, *"I am with you,"* meaning, "If anyone works for Me, I will be with him." This is true of the minister, the missionary, and every believer who works for Jesus. The presence of Jesus is intimately connected with work for Him.

You may be saying, "I never thought of that before. I work for Him on Sunday, but during the week I am not working for Him." You cannot have the presence of Jesus and let this continue to be the case. I do not believe that you can have the presence of Jesus all week and yet do nothing for Him. Therefore, my advice is, work for Him who is worthy, and His blessing and His presence will be found in the work. It is a blessed privilege to work for Christ in this perishing world. Oh, why is it that our hearts often feel so cold and closed up, and that so many of us say, "I do not feel *called* to Christ's work"? Be willing to yield yourself for the Lord's service, and He will reveal Himself to you.

Christ Is Completely for Us

Christ comes with His extraordinary promise, and He says to all believers: *"Lo, I am*

with you alway.' This is My promise. This is
what I can do in My power. This is what I
faithfully pledge to do. Will you receive it? I
give Myself to you."

To each person who comes to Him, Christ
says, "I give Myself to you, to be absolutely and
wholly yours every hour of every day, to be
with you and in you every moment, to bless
you and sustain you, and to give you the continual knowledge of My presence. I will be
wholly, wholly, wholly, yours."

We Are to Be Completely for Christ

In addition, the other side of it is that He
wants us to be wholly His. Are you ready right
now to take this as your motto: "Wholly for
God"? Let us fall down at His feet in true humility and heartfelt worship. O God, breathe
Your presence into our hearts so that You may
shine forth from our lives.

A missionary from Africa said that he has
often been touched by seeing how the native
Christians, when they give their hearts to Jesus, do not stand or kneel in prayer, but lie
down with their foreheads to the ground and
cry out to God with loud voices. I sometimes
wish that more Christians would do that.
However, we do not need to do it literally. Let

us do it in spirit, for the everlasting Son of God has come into our hearts.

Are you going to receive Him and cherish Him in your heart, to give Him glory and let Him have His way? Say, "I will seek You with my whole heart. I am wholly Yours." Yield yourself entirely to Him so that He has complete possession of you. He will take you and keep you in His possession. Jesus delights in the worship of His beloved. Our whole lives can become one continuous act of worship and work, filled with love and joy, if we will only remember and value what Jesus has said: *"Lo, I am with you alway, even unto the end of the world."*

Three

The Power of the Cross

The Power of the Cross

Christ, who through the eternal Spirit offered
himself without spot to God.
    —Hebrews 9:14

Once we fully commit our lives to Jesus, to live completely for Him, we need to understand a new dimension of life in Christ: the power of the Cross.

The Cross of Christ is the highest expression of the Spirit of Christ. The obedience and self-denial that Christ demonstrated when He endured the Cross are His chief characteristics. They are what distinguish Him from everyone in heaven and earth, and what give Him His glory as Mediator on the throne throughout eternity. Until we truly know the Spirit who led Christ to the Cross, we neither truly know Christ nor the Cross.

Moreover, once we have come to know the nature of the Spirit who led Christ to the

Cross, we will see that this knowledge is only one aspect of the great subject of the Spirit of the Cross. We will see how the Holy Spirit of Pentecost and the Spirit of the Cross are one and the same. The Holy Spirit led Christ to the Cross, and He also flows forth from the Cross to us as its purchase, and to whom its power is given.

We will then further find that as the Spirit led Christ to the Cross, and the Cross led to the giving of the Spirit, so the Spirit will always lead back to the Cross again, because He alone can reveal its meaning and communicate its fellowship. In other words, the Spirit led Christ to the Cross, and the Cross leads Christ and us to the outpouring of the Spirit, and the Spirit leads us back to the Cross.

The Cross, Our Life

The Scriptures do not teach us that when Christ bore the Cross and fulfilled the Atonement, the meaning of the Cross was exhausted. They do not indicate that when we trust in the finished work of the Cross, our only relationship to it is one of grateful confidence in what it has accomplished for us. No, the Word of God tells us that in the most intimate spiritual fellowship, the way of the Cross is to be our life. We are to live as if we have been crucified with Christ, which we have been. We are to walk as those who have crucified the flesh and who can conquer it in no other way but by continually regarding it as crucified. We are to take up our cross day by day, and to glory in it. Every moment of our lives, our relationship to the world is to be that of those who are crucified to it, and who know and believe that the world is crucified to them.

Therefore, if the nature of the Cross is to produce and characterize the only true Christian life, and if we are to have the same attitude toward the Cross that Jesus had, we need to know what it was that made the Spirit of the Cross the only power by which Christ could gain life for us or by which we can possess and enjoy life in Him.

In the first place, the path in which Jesus Christ walked did not derive its value from the amount of suffering it required or from His actual surrender to death, but from the mindset that motivated Him. That mindset was not something strange or different that came to Him in His last hour. It was what motivated and inspired Him throughout the whole course of His earthly life. And it is only as this perspective becomes the animating principle of the life of the believer that the thought of being *"crucified with Christ"* (Gal. 2:20) can have anything like true meaning. How did our Lord have *"this mind"* (Phil. 2:5) that was in Him, and the power to carry it out at any cost? We have the answer in our text for this chapter: *"Who through the eternal Spirit offered himself without spot to God."*

It was this Eternal Spirit who was in Christ from His birth, who taught Him to say words that contained the seed of His obedience and self-denial on the cross: *"I must be about my Father's business"* (Luke 2:49). It was this Spirit who led Christ to humble Himself and be treated as a sinner by being baptized in the Jordan River by John (Matt. 3:13–15). It was this Spirit who descended on Jesus like a dove to prepare Christ for the death for which He was set apart (vv. 16–17). It was this Spirit who led our Lord into the wilderness to resist and overcome and begin the struggle that ended on Calvary (Matt. 4:1). It was through this Spirit that He was led, step by step, to speak of and to face and to bear all He had to suffer.

Through the prophets, *"the Spirit of Christ...testified beforehand the sufferings of Christ"* (1 Pet. 1:11). In the same way, it was through the Eternal Spirit that all was fulfilled and accomplished. The Spirit of God, dwelling in flesh, leads inevitably and triumphantly to the Cross.

The Cross is the perfect expression of the mind of the Spirit—of what He asks and works. When God took possession of human nature to free it from sin and fill it with Himself, the only way He could do it was by slaying it. In the whole universe, there is no possibility of freedom from the power of sin except by personal separation from it through entire death to it. What God demands, the Spirit works. He worked His will in the Man Christ Jesus, the spotless Holy One who, because of His union with us and because He was our forerunner in the path of life, needed to die to sin. He works His will now as the Spirit of Christ who dwells in each believer.

The Crucifixion Spirit

Let us who desire to be filled with the Spirit consider the nature of the Spirit of the Cross. The Spirit leads us to a death that is characterized by the Cross. Since He had nothing higher than this to accomplish for us in Christ before He raised Jesus from the dead, He also has no higher work He can do for us than to lead us into the perfect fellowship of the Cross. Pray to know what this means.

Have you truly yielded to the Spirit so that He may lead you, as He led Christ, in the path of the Cross? Are you seeking the fullness of the Spirit in total agreement with His one purpose: to manifest in you the obedience and self-denial of Christ? For you, as it was for Jesus, the path of the Cross is the sure, the only path, to glory.

Deny Yourself and Take Up Your Cross

There is a deep and intimate connection between taking one's cross and following Christ. An additional aspect of crossbearing may be drawn from the words of Christ:

> If any man will come after me, let him deny himself, and take up his cross daily, and follow me. For whosoever will save his life shall lose it: but whosoever will lose his life for my sake, the same shall save it. (Luke 9:23–24)

A believer must *"deny himself"* before he can take up his cross and follow Christ. The deepest root of crossbearing and following Christ is exposed in this passage of Scripture. Even while the Christian is striving earnestly to follow Christ, and in some measure to take up his cross, there is a secret power that resists and opposes and prevents him. The very person who is praying and vowing and struggling to follow fully what his desire and will and heart are apparently set on, in his innermost self, refuses the cross to which his Lord has called him. Self, the real center of his being, the controlling power, refuses to accept it. And so, Christ teaches us that we must begin with the total denial of self.

The Cross Means Surrender

Taking up one's cross means accepting and surrendering to death. Self, the real inner life of a person, must die. For us to attempt to take up our cross and follow Jesus will mean unceasing failure unless we start with Christ's words: *"Let him deny himself, and take up his cross….Whosoever will lose his life for my sake, the same shall save it"* (Luke 9:23–24).

Christ calls me to love nothing more than I love Him, to lose my life, to disallow what gives life its own value, to disclaim what I am in my own person—to deny myself. Why must I first carry my cross and then be "crucified" on it? And why, if Jesus has already died for me on the cross and won life for me, must I still die, deny myself, and take up my cross daily?

Why the Cross?

The answer is simple, and yet it is not easy to comprehend. The real spiritual answer will be revealed only to the person who consents to obey Jesus before he understands what it all means. Through the sin of Adam, the life of mankind fell from its high position. It had been a vessel in which God caused His power and blessedness to work. But man fell under the power of the world, in which the god of this world has his rule and dominion.

Therefore, man has become a creature who has a strange, unnatural, worldly life. The will of God, heaven, and holiness, for which man was created, have become darkened and lost to him. The pleasures of the flesh and of the world and of self, which are the dark, accursed workings of the Evil One, have become natural and attractive. People do not see, they do not know, how sinful, wretched, and deadly they are—that they are alienated from God and that they bear within them the very seeds of hell. And this self, this innermost root of man's life, which he loves so much, is really the concentration of all that is not of God but is of the Evil One. Exhibiting a great deal of what is naturally beautiful and seemingly good, the power of self and its pride corrupt everything. They are the very seat of sin and death and hell.

Yet, once a person has consented to a life of the entire denial of self, he will welcome and love the cross. He will recognize it as the appointed power of God for freeing him from the evil power that is the only thing hindering him from being fully conformed to the image of God's Son—from loving and serving the Father as Christ did. To deny self is a work of the inner spirit. Taking the cross is the manifestation of this work.

"Let him deny himself, and take up his cross daily, and follow me" (Luke 9:23). When we receive insight into what the denial of self means, it becomes clear why the cross must be taken up *daily*. Taking up one's cross is not only called for during a time of special trial or suffering. During times of quiet and prosperity, the need is even more urgent. Self is the enemy that is always near and always seeking to regain its power.

For example, when the apostle Paul came down from the third heaven (see 2 Corinthians 12:2–7), he was in danger of being prideful. Yet, the danger of pride is always with us. Denying self and bearing the cross are to be everyday attitudes. When Paul said, *"I am crucified with Christ"* (Gal. 2:20) and, *"God forbid that I should glory, save in the cross of our Lord Jesus Christ, by whom the world is crucified unto me, and I unto the world"* (Gal. 6:14), he spoke of himself as living the crucifixion life each moment of the day.

There used to be a picture of a hand holding a cross, with the motto, "Teneo et Tenem"—"I hold and am held," or to use a looser translation, "I bear and am borne." The words Jesus used before His death, *"Take up* [your] *cross"* (Luke 9:23), reflect the first idea of the motto, "I hold." Accept your cross and bear it. Paul's words in Galatians, which were inspired by the Holy Spirit after Christ had been glorified—*"crucified with Christ"* (2:20)— point more to the second part of the motto: believe that His Cross, rather, that He, the Crucified One, bears you.

Before the work of the Cross was actually finished, the idea was to take up one's cross. Now that the finished work has been revealed, that is, taken up and transformed into the higher idea of being crucified with Christ, the concept is that I both bear the cross and am borne by Christ. *"I am crucified with Christ"* and *"Christ liveth in me"* (Gal. 2:20). It is only in the power of being borne by Christ that I can bear the cross.

Focus on Christ

What was first a condition that we had to fulfill if we were to follow Jesus, became the blessed fruit of following Him. When we hear the call, *"Follow me"* (Matt. 4:19), we think chiefly of all it implies for us. It is necessary that we do so, but it is not the chief thing. As we think of denying ourselves and taking up our cross daily, we realize how little we know of what it all means, and how little we are able to perform even what we do know.

A trusted leader takes all the responsibility for the journey and makes every provision. We need to focus our hearts on Jesus, who calls us to take up our cross and to follow Him. On Calvary, He opened the way for us and led us even to the throne of God's power. Yes, let us focus our hearts on Him. As He led His disciples, He will lead us.

The Cross is a mystery. Taking up one's cross is a deep mystery. To be *"crucified with Christ"* (Gal. 2:20) is the deepest mystery of redemption. The hidden wisdom of God is a mystery. Let us follow Christ with a true desire to let Him lead us. Let us live as fully as He did, to the glory of the Father. And let us enter with Christ through death into the fullness of life.

Four

Drawing Near to God

Drawing Near to God

For Christ also hath once suffered for sins, the just for the unjust, that he might bring us to God.
—1 Peter 3:18

In the last chapter, I described how the way of the Cross is the pathway to life in Christ. Now, I want to show you how the Cross enables us to draw near to God.

The Cross speaks of sin. It is only by comprehending the evil of sin, and fully admitting that it is hatred against God, that man can come to God. The Cross speaks of the Curse, which is God's judgment against sin. As long as man does not accept and affirm that God's judgment is righteous, there can be no thought of his being restored to God's presence. The Cross speaks of suffering. When we suffer, it is only as we accept the will of God and give up everything to that will that we can have union with God. The Cross speaks of death. It is only as man is ready to completely part with his whole present life—to die to it—that he can enter into, or fully receive to himself, the life and glory of God. Christ Himself did all this. His whole life was animated by the crucifixion spirit.

When Christ bore the Cross and entered into God's holy presence, He opened up a way in which we, too, could draw near to God. When He bore God's judgment for sin by His death, He *"put away sin"* (Heb. 9:26); He made an end of sin. By bearing the Curse, death, and condemnation, He carried away sin. He broke and abolished the power of the Devil, who had the power of death, and He set us free from Satan's prison.

The Cross and the blood and the death of Christ are God's assurance to the sinner that there is immediate acquittal and everlasting admission to God's favor and friendship for each one who will accept and entrust himself to the Savior. All the claims that God's law had against us and all the power that sin and Satan had over us are at an end. The death of Jesus destroyed sin and death. The path of the Cross is the path Christ has opened for us; in it, we have full freedom and power to draw near to God.

The path of the Cross is the only way that mankind can come to God. It is the path in which Christ Himself walked, the path that He opened for us, the path in which we, too, walk, and the only path in which we can lead others.

The Way of the Cross

The way of the Cross was the way in which Jesus, as Man, personally walked throughout His whole life, so that, as our Forerunner, He might enter in and appear before God for us.

> *Though he were a Son, yet learned he obedience by the things which he suffered; and being made perfect, he became the author of eternal salvation unto all them that obey him.* (Heb. 5:8–9)

The Cross was the path to God even for Jesus Himself. If there was no path to God for Christ except through death, the entire giving up of His life, how much more must this be the only path in which a sinner can come to be filled with the life of God. And now that Christ's death is an accomplished fact, the death and the life that we receive in Him are the power of His absolute surrender working in us, and this leads to the blessed indwelling of the Spirit. It is this kind of faith that enables a believer to say joyfully, *"I am crucified with Christ"* (Gal. 2:20) and, *"God forbid that I should glory, save in the cross of our Lord Jesus Christ, by whom the world is crucified unto me, and I unto the world"* (Gal. 6:14).

The crucifixion spirit, with its protest against and separation from the world, its sacrifice of all self-interest, and its absolute surrender to God, even to the death, characterizes the whole life and walk of a Christian. Daily bearing and glorying in the cross becomes, indeed, the path to God.

The Way to Bless Others

In this path, we can win others for Christ and bless them. It was as the Crucified One, giving His life for men, that Christ won the power to bless people. It was Peter's full acceptance of the sufferings that Christ underwent on His way to glory, of which he speaks in his first epistle, that filled the apostle with boldness to testify for his Lord. It was the intensity of Paul's desire for perfect conformity to his Lord's sufferings that gave him his power as an apostle.

The power of God's Spirit will work through the church in the measure in which God's people give themselves to Him as a sacrifice for men. It is Christ crucified who saves men. It is Christ crucified, living, and breathing in us who can and will use us for His saving work. Jesus living and working in us means precisely that we, like Him, are ready to give our lives for others. That means that we are to forget ourselves, to sacrifice ourselves, to suffer anything so that the lost may be won.

Life out of Death

At first, when a person enters into the truth of being *"crucified with Christ"* (Gal. 2:20) and of *"always bearing about in the body the dying of the Lord Jesus"* (2 Cor. 4:10), his chief thought is one of personal sanctification. He regards death to sin, death to the world, and death to self as the path of life and blessing.

But these desires cannot truly lead him to trust in Christ as the only One in whom death, and the life that arises out of this death, may be known and found, unless he understands another truth. He must also allow Christ to teach him the secret that every aspect of His obedience to the Father and His victory over sin was not for any personal glorification but was for the purpose of saving others around Him. The believer learns that the path of the cross cannot truly be followed by any who are not willing to work and to give their lives for others. The believer also learns, on the other hand, that the only true power to bless others comes when the cross, that is, death to the world and self, becomes the guiding principle of his daily life.

The cross was Christ's way to God—for Himself and for us. The cross is our way to God—for ourselves and for others. The cross is the way for us, so that it may be the way for others, too.

The church is continually speaking of needing to find the secret of power for its ministry of calling others to faith in Christ. People do not truly understand that the church only has power over the world when she is crucified to the world. The power is *"Christ crucified"* (1 Cor. 1:23); it is a *"stumblingblock"* and *"foolishness"* (v. 23) to men, but it is gloried in by those who can say, *"I am crucified with Christ"* (Gal. 2:20). The power of God manifests itself in preaching that proclaims the Cross of Christ, with its message of crucifixion to the world and self, and victory over sin and death.

The Enemy of the Cross

Now thanks be unto God, which always causeth us to triumph in Christ, and maketh manifest the savour of his knowledge by us in every place.

(2 Cor. 2:14)

When God created the earth, He placed Adam in Paradise, not only to work it, but to take care of it. It is evident that there must have been some evil power that Adam had to watch for and guard against. Since everything God created during the six days was very good, the evil must have been in existence previously. Scripture does not reveal how the evil came to exist or where it came from. It is enough for us to know that it existed and that it threatened the very center of the new creation—the Garden of God and the dwelling of man—with danger and destruction. It is as true today as it was then that God seeks to rob this evil of its power, and He purposes to do so through the medium of man.

The idea naturally suggests itself that man may have been created for the very purpose of conquering the evil that had existed before him. It is this perspective that establishes our apparently insignificant earth as the historic center of the universe. Satan, whose evil power had probably caused the formlessness (Gen. 1:2) or chaos of the earth, still sought to maintain his kingdom—in the very world that had been raised out of the ruins of his previous kingdom. It was on earth that man was created to conquer evil and to cast it out. This is what makes the world of such great importance in the eyes of God and His angels; it is the battlefield where heaven and hell meet in deadly conflict.

The terrible history of mankind can never be correctly understood until we allow Scripture to teach us that, even as God's purposes rule over all, there is, on the other hand, amid what appears to be nothing but natural growth and development, an organized system and evil kingdom that rules over men, keeps them in darkness, and uses them in its war against the kingdom of God's Son. On a scale that we can hardly imagine, through the slow length of ages that God's patience endures, amid all the freedom of human will and action, there is an unceasing contest going on. Though the outcome is not in question, the struggle is long and destructive. And in the history of that struggle, the Cross is the turning point.

The Cross Is a Triumph

Blotting out the handwriting of ordinances that was against us, which was contrary to us, and took it out of the way, nailing it to his cross; and having spoiled principalities and powers, he made a show of them openly, triumphing over them in it. (Col. 2:14–15)

The above Scripture wonderfully clarifies what the redemption of the Cross means. Having thrown off from Himself the principalities and powers, Christ made a show of them openly, triumphing over them in His Cross. The powers of darkness had made their onslaught in the darkness of the Cross; together, they had pressed on Him with everything that is terrible in their power, surrounding Him with the very darkness and misery of hell. They had formed a cloud so thick and dark that the very light of God's face was hidden from Him. But He defeated them; He beat back His enemies and overcame the temptation. He made a show of them openly; throughout the entire spiritual realm, before angels and devils, it was known that He had conquered.

When Christ died on the cross, the very grave gave up its dead (Matt. 27:52–53). And so

He triumphed over our enemy, death. In the spiritual world, the Cross is the symbol of victory. He led the principalities and powers in triumph as prisoners. Their power was broken forever, the gate of the prison in which they held men captive was broken open, and freedom was proclaimed to all their prisoners.

The Prince of this world has been cast out. He no longer has power to hold in bondage those who long for deliverance. He now only rules over those who consent to be his slaves. There is now a perfect deliverance for all who yield themselves to Christ and His Cross.

The great lesson of the second chapter of Colossians is that the Cross is a triumph. It began when Christ cried, *"It is finished"* (John 19:30). That was the beginning of a triumphal procession in which Christ moves on through the world in hidden glory, leading *"captivity captive"* (Eph. 4:8), leading His ransomed ones into liberty. And the believer can now continually rejoice, *"Now thanks be unto God, which always causeth us to triumph in Christ"* (2 Cor. 2:14). Every thought of the Cross, every step we take under the Cross, every proclamation of the Cross ought to have the tone of divine triumph: *"Death is swallowed up in victory....Thanks be to God, which giveth us the victory through our Lord Jesus Christ"* (1 Cor. 15:54, 57).

Without this mindset, our understanding of the meaning of the Cross and our experience of the power of the Cross will be defective. We will find this to be true both in our personal lives and in our work for others. In our personal lives, we will consider the cross to be a burden. The call to carry the cross will seem like a law that is hard to obey. Our attempts to live the crucifixion life will be a failure. The thought of a daily death will be wearisome. Crucifying the flesh demands such unceasing watchfulness and self-denial that we will give it up as a hopeless or fruitless task.

It cannot be otherwise until we know, in some measure, that the Cross is a triumph. We do not have to crucify the flesh. This has been accomplished in Christ. The act of crucifixion on Calvary is a finished transaction; the life and Spirit that go forth from the Crucifixion work with unceasing power. Our calling is to believe, to *"be of good cheer"* (John 16:33). Nothing less than His death can meet our need; nothing less than His death is at our disposal. *"Thanks be unto God, which always causeth us to triumph in Christ"* (2 Cor. 2:14).

It is of no less importance, in our service in the world, that we believe in the triumph of the Cross over the powers of darkness. Nothing except insight into this truth can teach us to know the supernatural strength and spiritual subtlety of our Enemy. Nothing else can teach us what our purpose must be as we *"wrestle...against the rulers of the darkness of this world"* (Eph. 6:12). That purpose is to bring men out of the world and away from the power of its Prince.

Nothing except this insight into the triumph that the Cross has won, and continually gives, can make us take our true position as the instruments and servants of our conquering King, servants whose one hope is to be led in triumph in Him. And nothing else can keep alive in us the courage and the hope that we need in our helplessness, as the mighty powers of the Enemy continually force themselves on us.

In faith, we must learn to say, through all our service and warfare, *"Thanks be unto God, which always causeth us to triumph in Christ"* (2 Cor. 2:14). The Cross, with its foolishness and weakness, its humiliation and shame, is the everlasting sign of the victory that Christ has won by mighty weapons that are spiritual, not carnal (2 Cor. 10:4). It is also the symbol of the victory that the church and every servant of Christ can continually win as we enter more deeply into the character of our crucified Lord, and, in this way, yield more fully to Him.

Five

Called into His Light

Called into His Light

But God forbid that I should glory, save in the cross of our Lord Jesus Christ, by whom the world is crucified unto me, and I unto the world.
—Galatians 6:14

There is no question that is of greater interest to the church today than that which deals with her relationship to the world. The meaning of the word *world,* as Christ used it, is simple. He used the expression to describe mankind in its fallen state and its alienation from God. He regarded it as an organized system or kingdom, the very opposite and mortal enemy of His kingdom. A mighty, unseen power, the *"god of this world"* (2 Cor. 4:4), rules it; and a spirit, the *"spirit of the world"* (1 Cor. 2:12), pervades it and gives it strength.

More than once, Christ revealed this as His special characteristic: *"I am not of this world"* (John 8:23). He also clearly taught His disciples, *"Ye are not of the world"* (John 15:19). He warned them that because they were not of the world, the world would hate them as it had hated Him (vv. 18–19). Of His sufferings, He said, *"The prince of this world cometh, and hath nothing in me"* (John 14:30); *"This is* [the] *hour, and the power of darkness"* (Luke 22:53); and, *"Be of good cheer; I have overcome the world"* (John 16:33).

In the hatred that nailed Him to the cross, the world revealed its true spirit, which is under the power of its god. In the Cross, Christ revealed His Spirit and His rejection of the world with all its threats and promises. The Cross is the confirmation of His word—that His kingdom *"is not of this world"* (John 18:36). The more we love the Cross and live by it, the more we will know what the world is and be separate from it.

The difference and antagonism between the two kingdoms is irreconcilable. No matter how much the world might be externally changed by Christian influence, its nature will remain the same. No matter how close and apparently favorable the alliance between the world and the church might become, the peace will be merely hollow and will last for only a time. When the Cross is fully preached—with its revelation of sin and the Curse, with its claim to be accepted and taken up—the enmity may quickly be seen. No one can overcome the world unless he is born of God (1 John 5:4).

Glorying in the Cross

In Galatians 6:14, we see how clearly Paul recognized the enmity between the Cross and the world, and how boldly he proclaimed it: *"God forbid that I should glory, save in the cross of our Lord Jesus Christ, by whom the world is crucified unto me, and I unto the world."* He identified himself so strongly with the Cross that its relationship to the world was also his. The Cross separated Paul from the world.

The Cross is the sign that the world has condemned Christ. Paul accepted this; the world was crucified to him, and he was crucified to the world. The Cross is God's condemnation of the world. Paul understood that the world is condemned and under the Curse. The Cross forever separated Paul from the world in its evil nature. The Cross alone could be their meeting place and reconciliation. It was for this reason that he gloried in the Cross and

85

preached that it was the only power that could draw men out of the world to God.

The view that many Christians take is the opposite of the perspective of Christ and John and Paul. These Christians speak as if in some way the Curse has been taken off of the world, and that the nature of the world has somehow been softened. They think of educating and winning the world—by meeting it more than halfway—with offers of friendship. They believe that the work of the church is to permeate the world with a Christian spirit and to take possession of it. They do not see that the spirit of the world permeates the church and takes possession of it to a far greater extent. As a result of this, the offense of the Cross is done away with and the Cross is adorned with the flowers of earth so that the world is quite content to give it a place among its idols.

War with the Enemy

In war, there is no greater danger than to underestimate the power of the enemy. We must remember that the work of the church is a war, an unceasing battle:

For we wrestle not against flesh and blood, but against principalities, against

> *powers, against the rulers of the dark-*
> *ness of this world, against spiritual*
> *wickedness in high places.   (Eph. 6:12)*

The world is made up of sinful humanity, not a mere collection of individuals who are led on in their sin by blind chance. It is an organized force that is unknowingly animated by one evil power that fills it with its spirit; it is a power of darkness, led on by one leader, the *"god of this world"* (2 Cor. 4:4).

> *Wherein in time past ye walked accord-*
> *ing to the course of this world, according*
> *to the prince of the power of the air, the*
> *spirit that now worketh in the children*
> *of disobedience.   (Eph. 2:2)*

It is only when the church accepts this truth in all its ramifications that she becomes capable of understanding the meaning of the Cross and how it was designed to draw men out of the world. And it is only in this aware-ness and acceptance that she will have the courage to believe that nothing but the persis-tent preaching of the Cross, in all its divine mystery, is what can overcome the world and save men out of it. The powers of the other world, the *"spiritual wickedness in high places"* (Eph. 6:12), working on earth in men, can only be conquered and brought into subjection by a higher power, the power of Christ, who, *"having spoiled principalities and powers ...made a show of them openly, triumphing over them in* [the Cross]" (Col. 2:15). It is the Cross, with its victory over sin and the Curse and death, with its love and life and triumph, that alone is the power of God.

Blinded Minds

The great power of the world lies in its darkness. The Scriptures tell us, *"The god of this world hath blinded the minds of them which believe not"* (2 Cor. 4:4) and, *"We wrestle not against flesh and blood, but against principalities, against powers, against the rulers of the darkness of this world"* (Eph. 6:12). If anything of the spirit of this world is found in individual believers—or the church—then, to the same extent, they will be incapable of seeing things in the light of God. They will judge spiritual truth with a heart that is prejudiced by the spirit of the world that is in them.

No person, no matter how honest his intentions are, no matter how earnest his thoughts are, no matter how much intellectual power he has, can understand and receive God's truth any farther than the Spirit of Christ and the Cross has expelled—or is truly sought after to expel—the spirit of the world in him. The Holy Spirit, when He is carefully waited on and yielded to, is the only Light that can open the eyes of the heart to see and to know what is of the world and what is of God. Moreover, we only truly yield to the Holy Spirit when the path of the Cross, with its crucifixion of the flesh and the world, becomes the law of our lives. The Cross and the world are diametrically and unchangeably opposed to one other.

Sin brought about destruction and ushered in the spirit of the world. Man was to have lived on earth in the power of the heavenly life, in fellowship with God, and in obedience to His will. When man sinned, he fell entirely under the power of this *"present evil world"* (Gal. 1:4), which the god of this world rules and uses as a means of temptation and sin. Man's eyes were closed to eternal and spiritual things, and things related to time and the physical world mastered and ruled him.

Some Christians speak as if the Cross of Christ has taken away the Curse and the power of sin in the world in such a way that the believer is now free to enter into the enjoyment of the world without danger. They believe that the church now has the calling and power of appropriating the world—of taking possession of it for God.

This is certainly not what Scripture teaches. The Cross removes the Curse from the believer, not from the world. Whatever has sin in it, has the Curse on it as much as ever. What the believer is to possess of the world and its goods must first be *"sanctified by the word of God and prayer"* (1 Tim. 4:5).

Nothing except an understanding of the evil of the spirit of the world, and our deliverance from it by the Cross and the Spirit of Christ—nothing except the Spirit and power of the Cross animating us, separating and freeing us from the spirit of the world—can keep us so that we are in the world but not of it. It cost Christ His agony in the Garden of Gethsemane, where He sweat blood; His awful struggle with death; and the sacrifice of His life, to conquer the world by the Cross. Nothing less than a full and wholehearted entrance into fellowship with Him in His crucifixion can save us from the spirit of the world.

Crucified with Christ

In the epistle to the Galatians, there are several passages that refer to the Cross of Christ, but only one of them speaks definitely of the Atonement: *"Christ hath redeemed us from the curse of the law, being made a curse for us"* (3:13). The other passages in Galatians pertain to fellowship with the Cross and its relationship to our inner life. When Paul says, *"I am crucified with Christ: nevertheless I live; yet not I, but Christ liveth in me"* (2:20); *"They that are Christ's have crucified the flesh"* (5:24); and, *"The world is crucified unto me, and I unto the world"* (6:14), he speaks of a life, an inward disposition, a spiritual experience, in which the same Spirit and power that sustained Christ when He bore the Cross, are maintained and manifested in the believer.

There are many who claim to boast, or glory, in the Cross (v. 14). They consider their faith in the righteousness of Christ as man's justification before God to be the great proof of their faithfulness to Scripture. Yet, in their toleration of things that are of the spirit of this world, and through their wholehearted enjoyment and participation in them, they prove that they do not really glory in a Cross that crucifies the world. To them, the Cross that atones and the world that crucified the Savior are at peace with one another. They do not know anything about walking the path of the Cross, which crucifies the world for being an accursed thing and keeps us crucified to it.

The Cross Will Prove Its Power

If the preaching of the Cross—not only for forgiveness but for holy living, not only for pardon from sin but for power over the world and an entire freedom from its spirit—is to be of central importance to the church today, as it was with the apostle Paul, we must implore God to reveal what He means by the world and what He means by the power of the Cross. It is in the lives of believers who are actually and obviously crucified to the world and all that is of it, that the Cross will prove its power.